Back to Basics

# SCIENCE

## for 7–8 year olds

Godfrey Hall

Letts

# Body parts

Inside our bodies there are many different parts. Some of these are called **organs**. Match the words with the organs.

stomach kidneys lungs heart brain

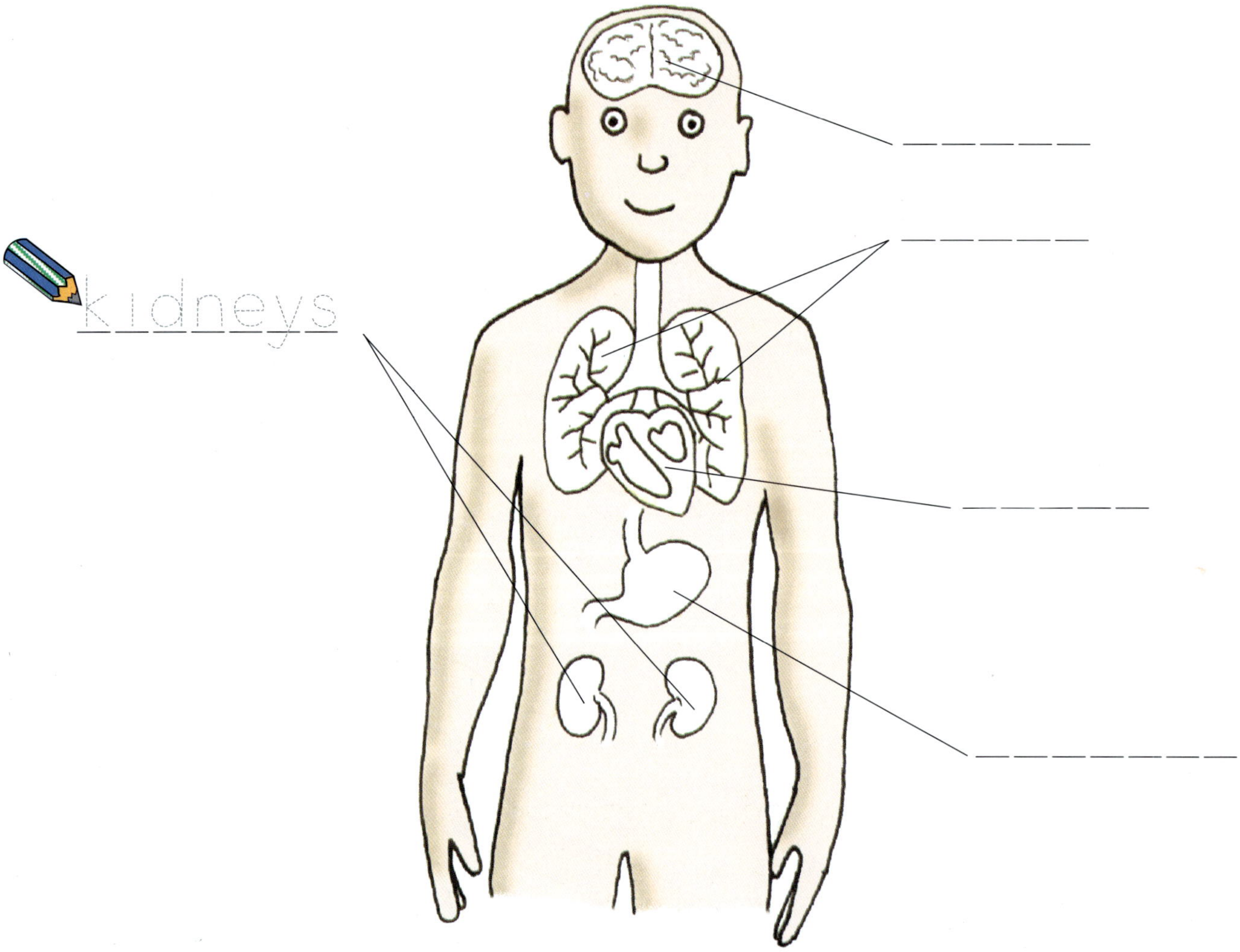


Join up the organs with the jobs they do.

| | |
|---|---|
| The kidneys | digests food. |
| The stomach | looks after thoughts, feelings and memory. |
| The lungs | filter blood. |
| The heart | pumps blood around the body. |
| The brain | breathe in air. |

# Teeth

Our teeth chop up and chew food before we swallow it.
We have three different types of teeth inside our mouths: **grinders**, **cutters** and **tearers.**

Fill in **grinder**, **cutter** or **tearer**.

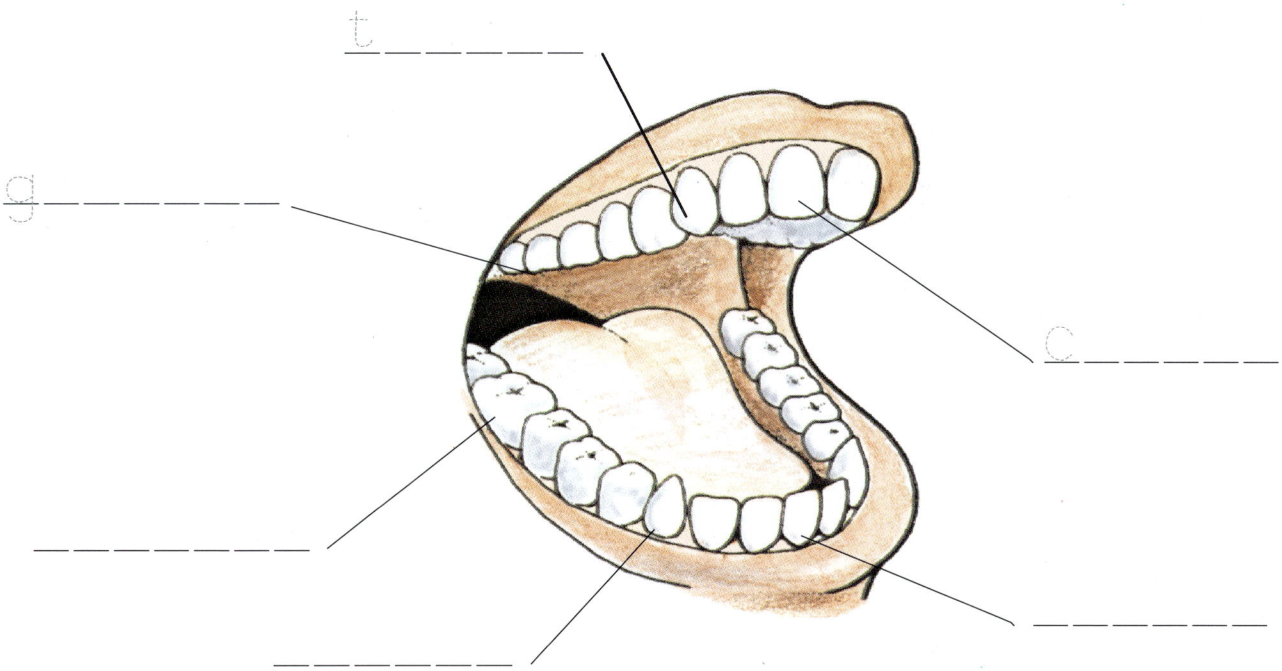


The three types of teeth are called: **molars**, **incisors** and **canines**.

**Molars** grind up our food before we swallow it.
**Canines** tear off pieces of food.
**Incisors** cut up our food.

Some animals use one type of tooth more than others to eat their food.
Fill in the right type of tooth.

Lions tear up meat. They have large __________.
Sheep grind up grass. They have large _________.
Beavers cut down trees. They have large____________.

# What our bodies need

If we are to keep fit and healthy we must eat a selection of different foods. Look at the list and use it to make up three sensible meals.

**Breakfast Menu**

**Lunch Menu**

**Dinner Menu**

| | |
|---|---|
| orange juice | squash |
| peas | toast |
| cheese | potatoes |
| bread | apple |
| carrots | corn flakes |
| yoghurt | tea |
| lettuce | grapefruit |
| | roast chicken |
| | tomatoes |

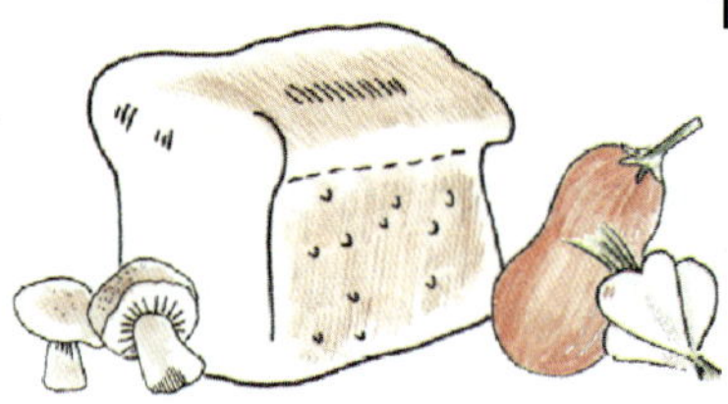

Underline the foods you can eat as much of as you like and ring the ones you should only eat a little of.

| | | | |
|---|---|---|---|
| fruit | cakes | sweets | vegetables |
| fried food | salad | biscuits | fizzy drinks |

# Same but different

Your fingerprints are different from everyone else's. So are your palm prints. Use an ink pad or a water-based paint and make a print of your left thumb and fingers of your left hand. Get a friend to do the same.

| | thumb | 1st finger | 2nd finger | 3rd finger | 4th finger |
|---|---|---|---|---|---|
| you | | | | | |
| a friend | | | | | |

Compare the results.

How do you think the police use fingerprints to catch criminals?

..........................................................................................

..........................................................................................

Here is a group of people.

Write down four things they all share.

.................... ....................

.................... ....................

Four differences.

.................... ....................

.................... ....................

# Creatures and their young

Match the adult creatures with their young. Fill in the baby creatures' names using the words below.

gosling foal cub kitten puppy calf

# Keeping things warm

Sometimes we need to keep things warm. The hot water tank in your home may have a jacket on to keep it warm. You may keep your drink warm in a special flask.

Look at the drawings below. Which of these materials will keep the drink warm? Put a tick ✔ or a cross ✘ in each box.

To test them, put some warm water into a plastic glass. Cover it round the outside with one of the materials. Put in a thermometer and leave it for 15 minutes. Does the temperature stay the same or drop?

The best material for keeping the drink warm is ..................................................

Test out some other materials.

# In reverse

When you heat or cool something you change the way it is. Some things can be changed back, others cannot. Look at the list below. Which of these things can be changed back? Tick ✔ the boxes.

| | yes | no |
|---|---|---|
| 1 boiling water | ✔ | ☐ |
| 2 frozen water | ☐ | ☐ |
| 3 a cooked egg | ☐ | ☐ |
| 4 a burnt piece of paper | ☐ | ☐ |
| 5 a baked cake | ☐ | ☐ |
| 6 melted butter | ☐ | ☐ |

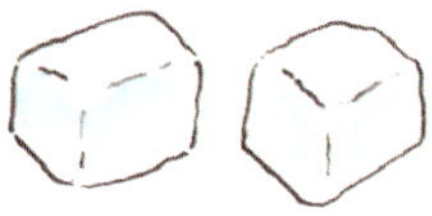

If something can be changed back, we say that it can be **reversed**.

Fill in **can** or **cannot** in these changes.

1 Ice cubes ______ be changed back into water.

2 A fried egg ______ be changed back into a raw egg.

3 Ash ______ be changed back into wood.

4 Steam ______ be changed back into water.

5 A cake ______ be changed back into flour, sugar, butter and eggs.

# Magnets

Each end of a magnet is called a **pole**. All magnets have a North and South Pole. The North Pole is often the red end and the South Pole the blue end.

Take two bar magnets. What happens when you push one end towards the other? Write by the side what happens if you....

1

2

3

4

If the magnets move towards each other we say they **attract**.

If they move away from each other we say they **repel**.

Fill in **repel** or **attract** in the spaces.

**1** North to North

**2** North to South

**3** South to South

**4** South to North

# How strong?

**Magnets** come in lots of different shapes and sizes. They can be used to pick things up or stick things together, such as cupboard doors. The strength of a magnet can depend on its size. Some large magnets are able to move old cars round scrap yards.

Take a horseshoe magnet. Stick a metal paper clip onto the end. Keep adding more until the end ones stop being attracted. How many paper clips can you pick up with your magnet? What else will it pick up?

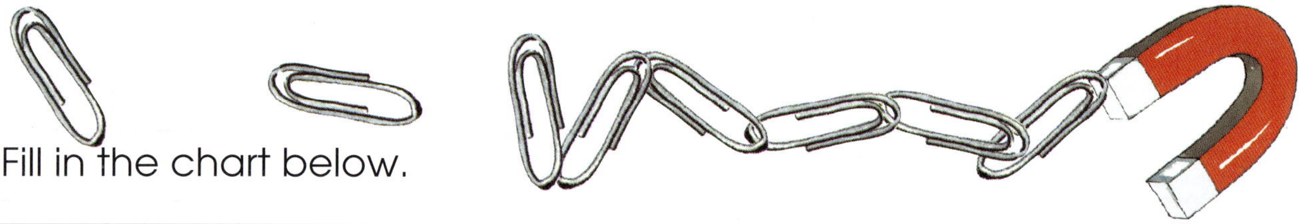

Fill in the chart below.

| Shape of magnet | Number of paper clips | Other things it picks up |
|---|---|---|
| | | |

What other ways can you think of to test your magnets?

..........

..........

..........

..........

# Waterproof

Look at the pictures below. If you were to go out in the rain, which of these hats would be best for keeping off the rain? Tick ✔ the boxes.

**1** newspaper

good ☐ bad ☐

**2** plastic

good ☐ bad ☐

**3** cardboard

good ☐ bad ☐

**4** wool

good ☐ bad ☐

**5** tissue paper

good ☐ bad ☐

**6** steel

good ☐ bad ☐

Test out plastic, paper, wool and cotton to see if they are waterproof. Put a tablespoon of water on each material. Record what happens.

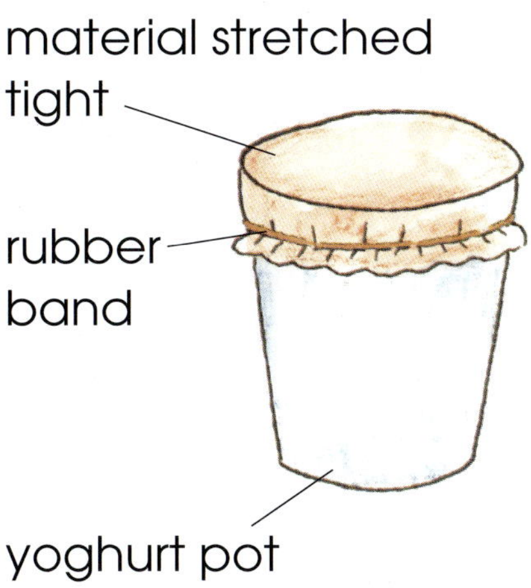


| Material | Waterproof? |
|---|---|
| plastic | |
| paper | |
| wool | |
| cotton | |

# Shadows

Look at the pictures below. Draw in where the **shadows** should be.

Make some shadows on the wall of a darkened room by getting a friend to shine a torch towards your hands. See what shapes you can make on the wall. Try these shapes. Can you think of others?

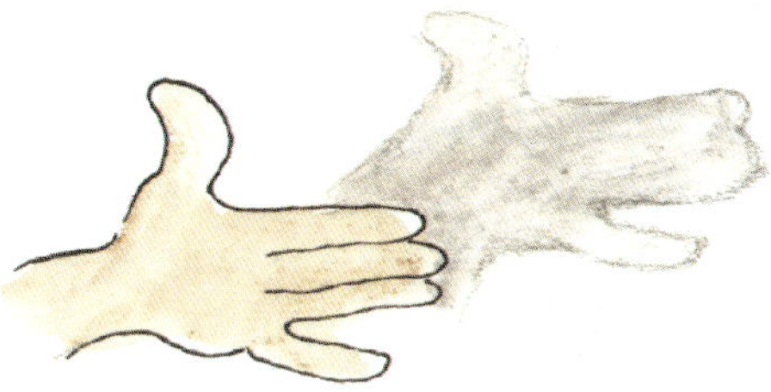

Try putting some different objects between the torch and the wall. What kind of shadows can you make?

# Rainbows

If you look at a waterfall with the sun behind you, you may see a rainbow in front of it. The sunlight has been split up by the spray. This is called the **spectrum**. It is made up of seven colours: red, orange, yellow, green, blue, indigo and violet.
Colour in the rainbow below.

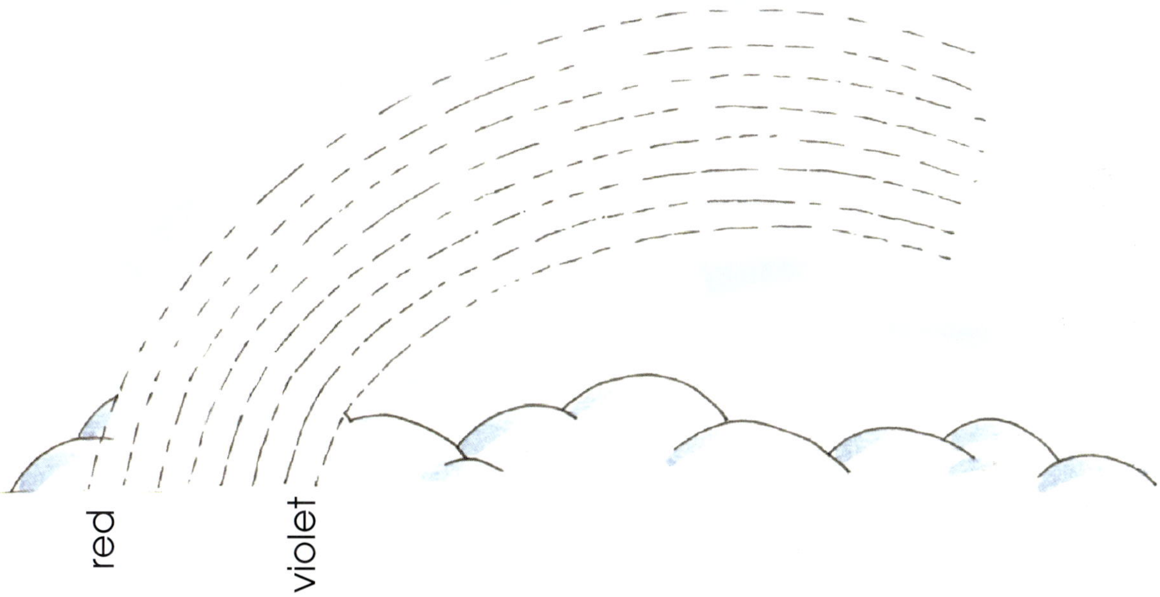


Learn this saying to help you remember the colours of the rainbow:

Richard Of York Gave Battle In Vain.

Cut out a card as shown and divide it into six. Colour in each section. Push a pencil through the middle and spin the card. What happens?

..............................................................................

..............................................................................

# How do they fly?

Look at the objects below. Write down by the side how they fly. Do these use **hot air**, an **engine**, the **wind** or their **own power**?

1 ……………………

2 ……………………

3 ……………………

4 ……………………

5 ……………………

6 ……………………

7 ……………………

8 ……………………

1
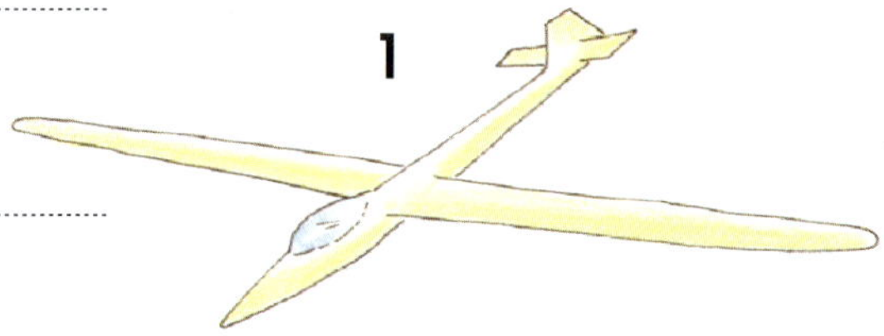

2
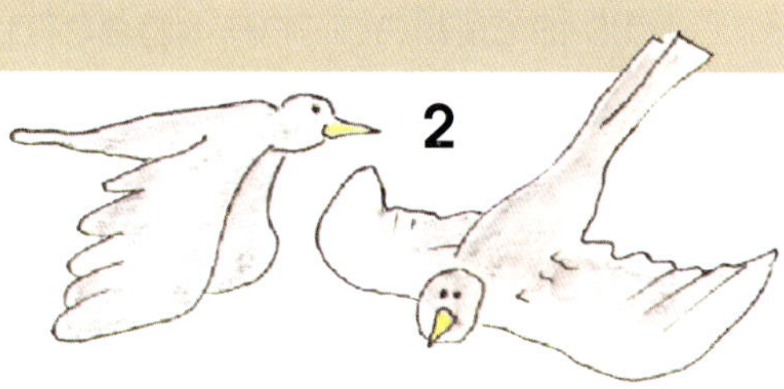

3
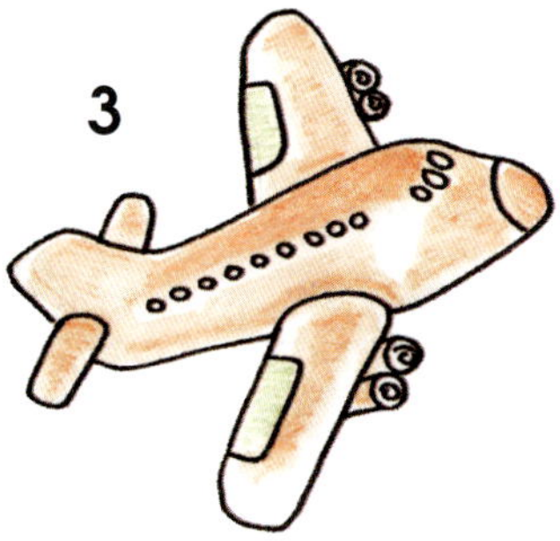

4
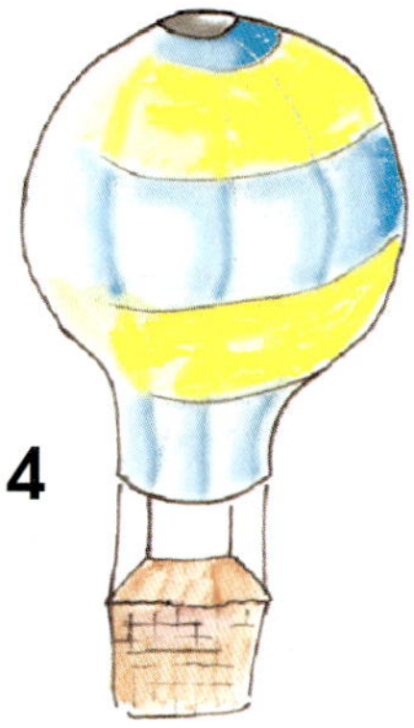

5

6

7

8

Unscramble these words.

**1** alenp _ _ _ _ _ **2** rdbi _ _ _ _ **3** btterlyfu _ _ _ _ _ _ _ _ _

**4** labolon _ _ _ _ _ _ _ **5** lyf _ _ _ **6** gldier _ _ _ _ _ _

# Make a parachute

Cut out a square of tissue paper with sides 15cm long. Stick a piece of cotton 18cm long to each corner. Join the ends of the cotton to a piece of plasticine.

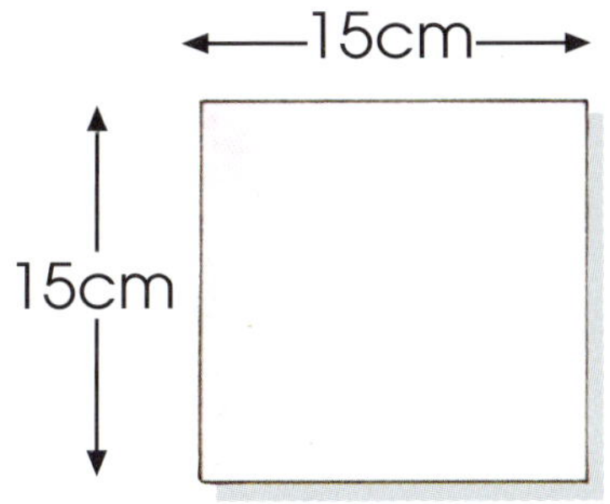

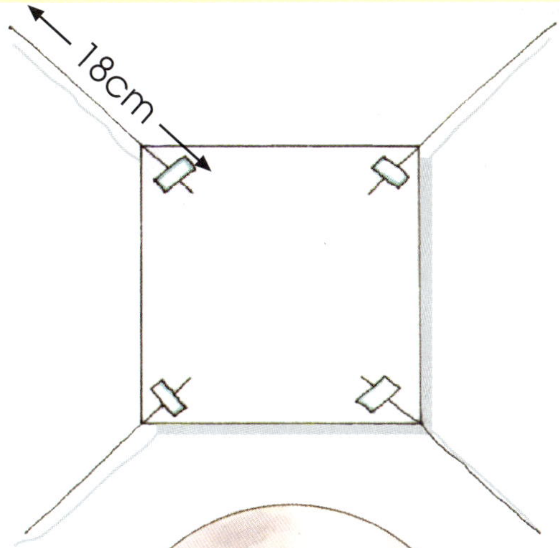


Stand on a chair or halfway up some stairs. Let your parachute fall.

Make some more parachutes from other materials. Fill in the chart below.

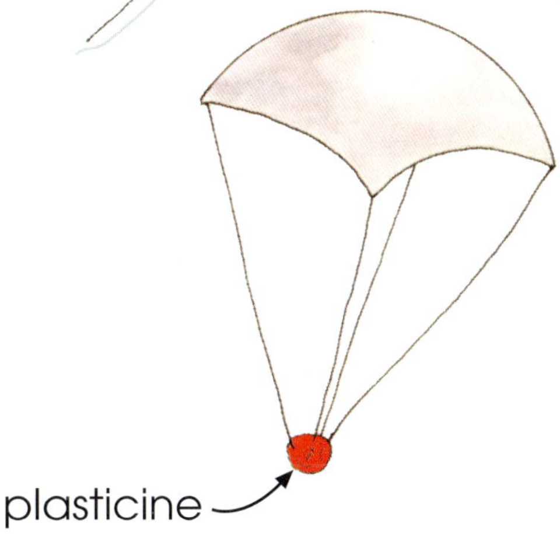


| Material | Did it make a good or bad parachute? |
|---|---|
| tissue paper | |
| cotton cloth | |
| newspaper | |
| plastic | |
| cardboard | |
| wool | |

# Simple recipes

It is very important to follow the instructions of a recipe. Look at these pictures. Put them into the right order by matching the pictures with the sentences. Write the numbers 1 to 5 in the boxes.

**A**

**B**

**C**

**D**

**E**

**F**

**1** Put 5 tablespoons of flour into a bowl.

**2** Add a little water.

**3** Mix it until you have a light mixture.

**4** Make it into a round shape.

**5** Put it onto a baking tray.

**6** Put it into a hot oven for 20 minutes.

# Boats

Make a simple boat from a margarine carton. Divide the inside into sections using some card.

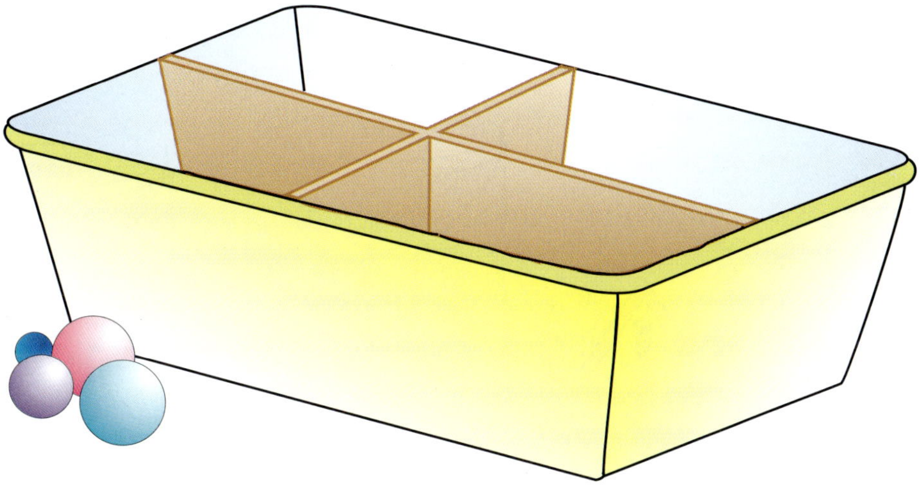

Put your boat on the water. Put some marbles or weights in one section. Record what happens. Now add weights to other sections.
Fill in the chart below.

| Your boat's load | What happens? |
| --- | --- |
| 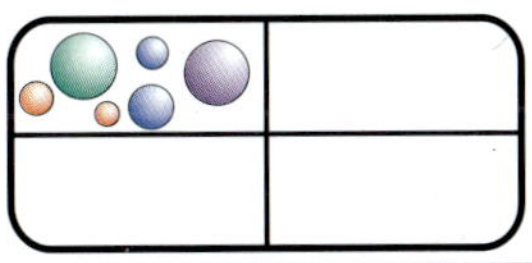 | |
| 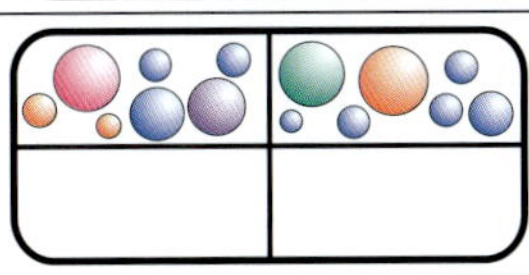 | |
| 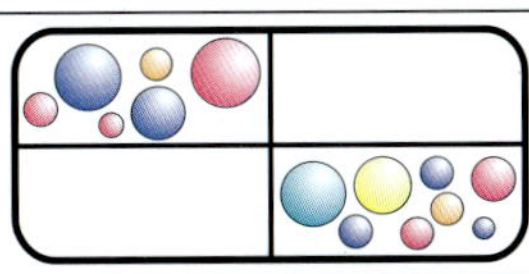 | |
| 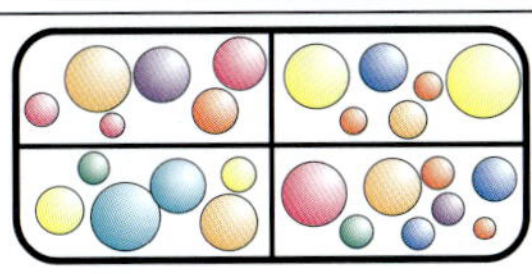 | |

How many marbles will your boat carry before it sinks?

# Rainfall gauge

Weather forecasters need to know how much rain falls in one place. To do this they use a **rainfall gauge**. This is a simple one you can make yourself.

Find a plastic bottle. Cut round the middle. Turn the top upside down to make a funnel. Use some sticky tape and mark a scale in centimetres on the outside. Put your rain gauge in the open. Use it to fill in the table below.

| Days | Centimetres of rain |
|---|---|
| 1 | |
| 2 | |
| 3 | |
| 4 | |
| 5 | |
| 6 | |
| 7 | |

How many centimetres of rain fell in one week? ☐ cm

# Electricity

Which of these electrical machines would you find in the **home**, in a **shop** and in an **office**? Tick ✔ the boxes.

1

2

3

4

5

| | home | shop | office |
|---|---|---|---|
| 1 | ☐ | ☐ | ☐ |
| 2 | ☐ | ☐ | ☐ |
| 3 | ☐ | ☐ | ☐ |
| 4 | ☐ | ☐ | ☐ |
| 5 | ☐ | ☐ | ☐ |

List five rules that you should remember when using something run by electricity.

1 Never touch a plug with wet hands

2 ..........

3 ..........

4 ..........

5 ..........

# Materials

Different materials are used for different jobs. Join up the materials with how they are used.

iron

plastic

cotton

wood

copper

wool

glass

Which of the materials above:

are hard ..........

will not rust ..........

are warm ..........

# Fruits and seeds

Fill in the spaces using the words in the box.

| | | | | |
|---|---|---|---|---|
| small | spins | mangoes | peaches | river |
| conkers | acorn | apples | fur | blown |

**1** The fruit of the oak tree is the .................................. .

**2** Horse chestnut seeds are called .................................. .

**3** Some fruits have pips in, fruits such as .................................. .

**4** Many seeds are .................................. by the wind.

**5** The sycamore seed .............................. to the ground.

**6** Some seeds get caught in the ........................ of an animal's coat.

**7** Seeds can fall into a .................................. or stream and travel long distances.

**8** Tropical plants include .................................. and paw paws.

**9** The seeds of the poppy are very .............................. .

**10** Some fruits are very soft when they are ripe.
These include .................................. and plums.

Make a collection of different fruits and seeds from the trees in your area.

# Light

Light will go through some materials. If this happens we say they are **transparent**. If light will not travel through a material, we call it **opaque**.

Test out these materials using a torch in a darkened room. Shine the torch at the material. Put a tick ✔ if it is transparent and a cross ✘ if it is opaque.

- [ ] glass
- [ ] water
- [ ] a woollen rug
- [ ] cooking oil
- [ ] a china cup
- [ ] a coin
- [ ] wood
- [ ] coloured plastic
- [ ] milk
- [ ] a leather glove
- [ ] tissue paper
- [ ] a cotton tea towel

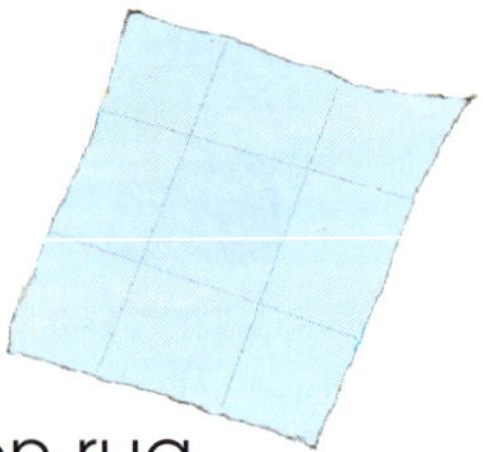
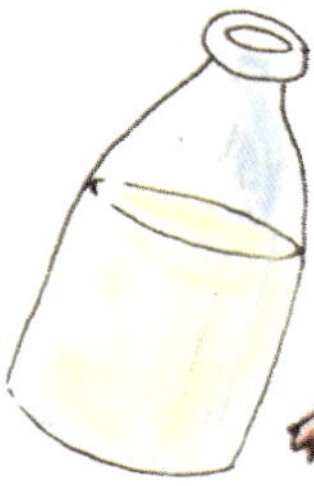

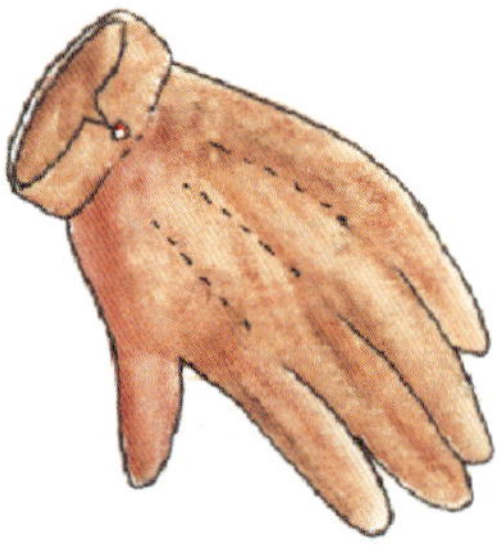

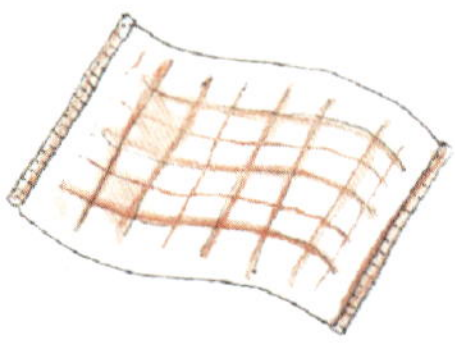

# Different stages

**Raw materials** are used to make things. Many have to go through different stages before they end up looking like a table or a book. Fill in the spaces in these chains.

**1**

sheep's wool

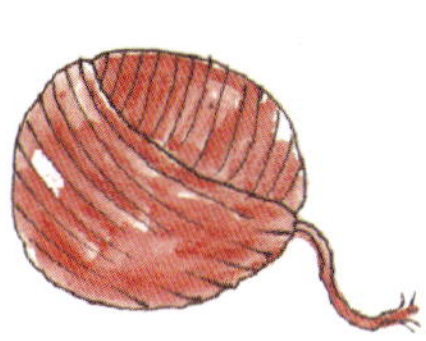
yarn

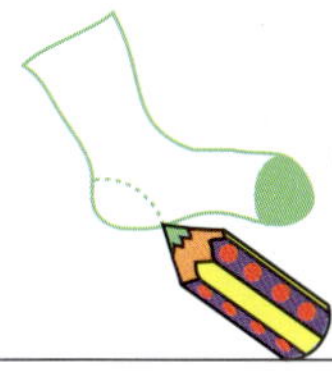

**2**

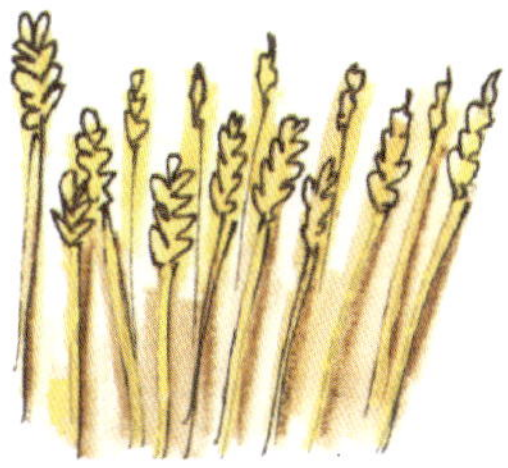
wheat

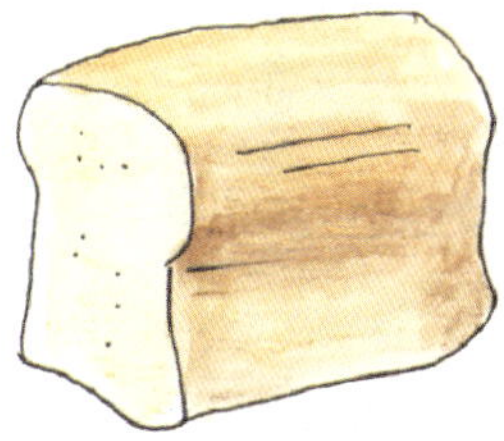
bread

**3**

bricks

wall

**4**

trees

wood

**5**

cow

butter

# Falling

Fill a tray with sand. Drop a marble into it. Look at the dent it has made. Smooth the sand over. Drop the marble from a height of 50cm, 100cm and 200cm. Does it make any difference to the size of the dent?

What did you find out?

........................................................................................................

........................................................................................................

Try dropping other objects into the sand. Does it make any difference if the object is hard or soft?

........................................................................................................

........................................................................................................

Drop two objects that are the same size but different weights onto the sand. Which lands first?

........................................................................................................

If you dropped a marble on to these materials would it make a large or a small dent? Write in **large** or **small**.

| | | | | | |
|---|---|---|---|---|---|
| **1** | flour | | **3** | sand | |
| **2** | clay | | **4** | steel | |

# Levers

**Levers** have been used for thousands of years. The simplest lever is shown below.

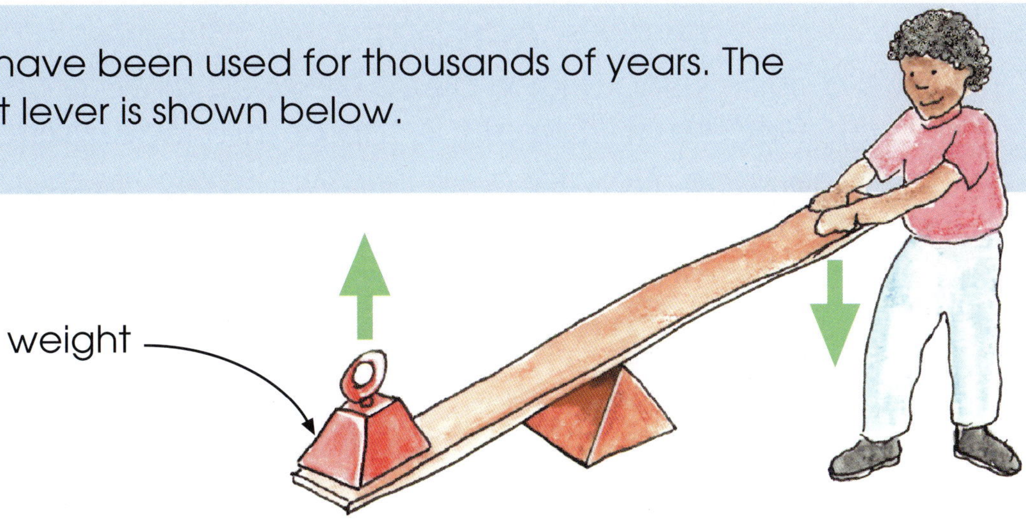


When the person pushes down at one end the weight will move upwards. If you open a tin of paint with a screwdriver you are using a simple lever. A bottle opener, a nutcracker and a wheelbarrow are all levers. Levers are a type of **machine**.

Tick ✔ the sentences you think are correct.

1 You can lift a book using a ruler and matchbox as a simple lever. ☐

2 A bottle opener is one kind of lever. ☐

3 Thousands of years ago people moved huge stones using levers. ☐

4 A screwdriver cannot be used as a lever. ☐

5 A seesaw acts as a lever. ☐

6 You can carry heavy loads in a wheelbarrow because it is a lever. ☐

7 A lever is a machine. ☐

# Friction

Make a slope using a long piece of wood or card and a book or brick. Place a marble at the top of the slope. Watch it roll down the slope. Now try a rubber. Which moves more easily? It should be the marble. This is because there is less **friction** between the marble and the slope. Marbles have a smooth shiny surface which reduces friction. Fill in the chart below.

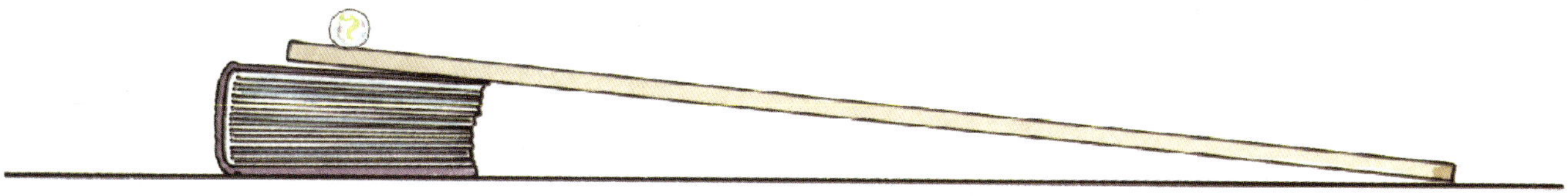

| Object | Does it move easily down the slope? |
|---|---|
| 1  |  |
| 2  | |
| 3  | |
| 4  | |
| 5  | |
| 6  | |
| 7 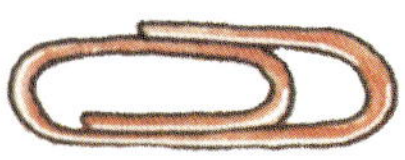 | |

Try rubbing soap onto the slope. Does it make any difference to your results?

# Dissolving

If you put a spoonful of sugar into a cup of tea and give it a stir the sugar should **dissolve**. The sugar has not disappeared. It is still there because we can taste it. Some things will dissolve and others will not.

Which of these will dissolve in cold water? Test them out by putting one teaspoon of each into a cup of water. Does it make any difference if you give it a stir?

| | **Does it dissolve?** | |
|---|---|---|
| | **Yes** | **No** |
| **1** sugar | | |
| **2** sand | | |
| **3** tea | | |
| **4** flour | | |
| **5** cooking oil | | |
| **6** washing-up liquid | | |
| **7** salt | | |

# A fair test

It is very important when you do a science experiment that your test is **fair**. Below are five experiments. How could you make sure that they are fair tests?

1 Checking the temperature outside everyday.

..................................................

..................................................

..................................................

2 Dissolving things in a cup of water.

..................................................

..................................................

..................................................

3 Checking the length of children's feet and arms.

..................................................

..................................................

..................................................

4 Measuring how fast a toy car travels down a slope.

..................................................

..................................................

..................................................

5 Finding out how high a ball bounces when it is dropped from different heights.

..................................................

..................................................

..................................................

# What happens next?

Look at the drawings below. Write down what you think **might** happen next.

**1**

Place some cress seeds on damp cotton wool on a sunny windowsill.

........................................

........................................

........................................

**2**

Bring the North and South Poles of two bar magnets together.

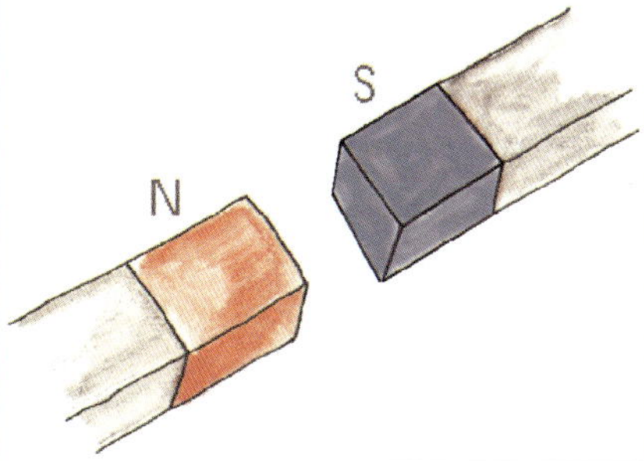


........................................

........................................

........................................

**3**

Join the two wires A and B together.

........................................

........................................

........................................

**4**

Push down on one end of seesaw.

........................................

........................................

........................................

**5**

Blow down the tube.

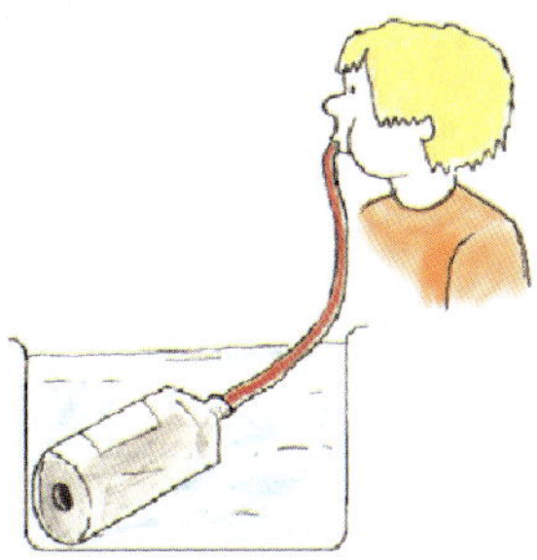

........................................

........................................

........................................

**6**

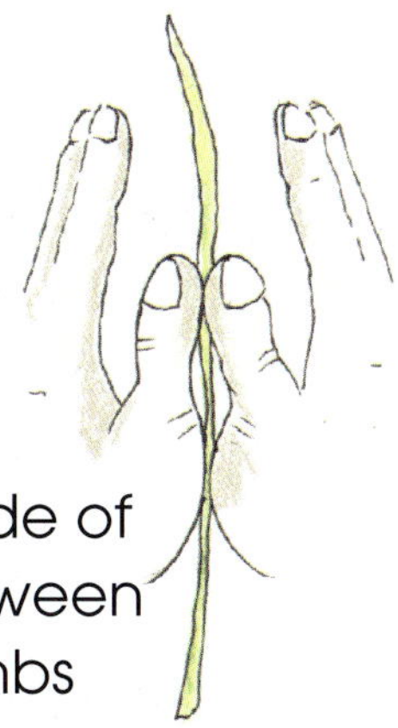

Put a blade of grass between your thumbs and blow.

........................................

........................................

........................................

# Insect watch

Join the name of the insect with what it looks like and where it lives.

hive

soil

leaf

pond

rotting log

bee

dragonfly

woodlouse

ant

caterpillar

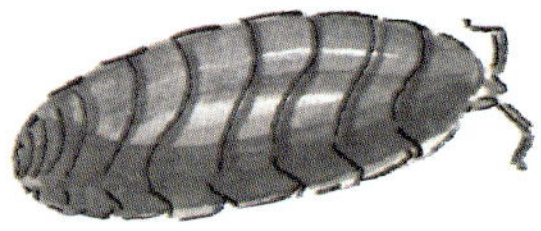

# Looking after our world

Match the sentences with the pictures above. Fill in 1 to 5 in the boxes.

1 We must try to throw less away.

2 The number of people in the world is getting bigger and bigger.

3 Fumes and smoke cause pollution.

4 Putting chemicals into rivers kills fish.

5 Cutting down the rainforests takes away creatures' homes.

6 Hunting rare animals means they will die out.

Write four ways you might be able to help look after the world.

1 ..............................

..............................

2 ..............................

..............................

3 ..............................

..............................

4 ..............................

..............................

# Answers

**To Parents:** We have not provided *all* the answers here. Some are examples only, as there are many possible correct answers. Use your judgement to see if your child's answer is a sensible alternative. Also, we have not given the answers to any practical activities. These will depend on the particular materials, etc, with which your child does the experiment so they will need to be checked by you.

### Page 2

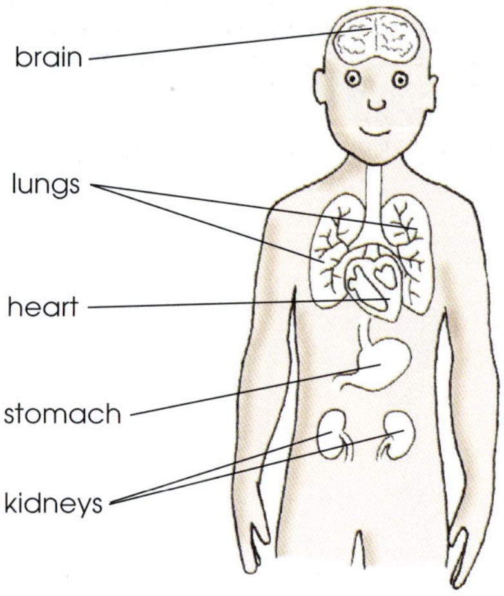


The stomach digests food.
The lungs breathe in air.
The heart pumps blood around the body.
The brain looks after thoughts, feelings and memory.

### Page 3

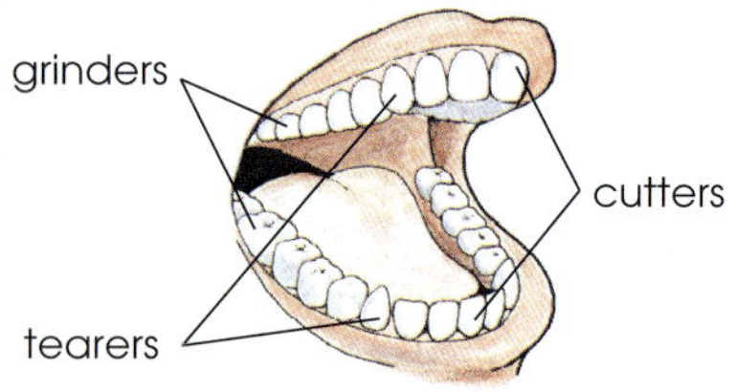


Lions have large canines.
Sheep have large molars.
Beavers have large incisors.

### Page 4

For example:
Breakfast: tea, toast, grapefruit, cornflakes.
Lunch: bread, lettuce, cheese, tomatoes, apple, squash.
Dinner: roast chicken, potatoes, peas, carrots, yoghurt, orange juice.

fruit salad vegetables
fried food biscuits cakes
sweets fizzy drinks

### Page 5

The police use fingerprints to identify criminals.
Share: all have 2 legs, arms, eyes, a nose, mouth, feet etc.
Differences: hair, eye and skin colour, boy or girl, straight or curly hair, glasses, height, clothes etc.

### Page 6

| | |
|---|---|
| horse/foal; | lion/cub; |
| goose/gosling; | dog/puppy; |
| cat/kitten; | cow/calf. |

### Page 7

Ticks: cotton, wool and newspaper.
Crosses: plastic, cardboard
The best material would be wool.

### Page 8

**1** yes; **2** yes; **3** no; **4** no; **5** no; **6** yes.
**1** can; **2** cannot; **3** cannot; **4** can; **5** cannot.

### Page 9

**1** The magnets come together.
**2** The magnets push away.
**3** The magnets come together.
**4** The magnets push away.

**1** repel; **2** attract; **3** repel; **4** attract.

### Page 10

Ways of testing a magnet include:
Stick on some paper clips and attach a magnet to the other end. Then have a tug of war to see which magnet is the strongest.
See how much a magnet can pull up a slope. The stronger the magnet the more it will be able to pull up the slope.
See how far away a magnet has to be before it will make a paper clip move. The further away it is the stronger the magnet.

### Page 11

**1** bad; **2** good; **3** bad; **4** bad; **5** bad; **6** good.
plastic - yes; paper - no; wool - no; cotton - no.

### Page 12

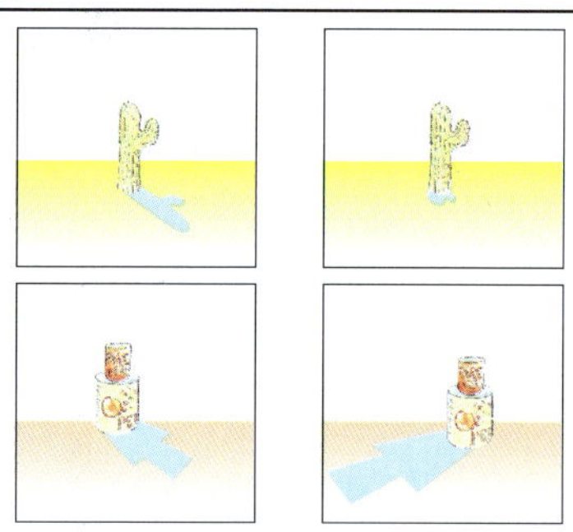

### Page 13

When the card spins round the colours should come together making white.

### Page 14

**1** wind; **2** own power; **3** engine; **4** hot air; **5** own power; **6** wind; **7** own power; **8** engine.
**1** plane; **2** bird; **3** butterfly; **4** balloon; **5** fly; **6** glider.

### Page 15

Probably the best parachutes will be made from cotton and plastic.

### Page 16

B1, D2, C3, A4, F5, E6.

### Page 17

When the weight is on one side the boat will probably tip over.
If the weight is on opposite corners the boat will be more stable.
The boat will be most stable if the weight is evenly distributed.

### Page 19

**1** home; **2** home; **3** shop; **4** home, shop and office; **5** office.
Never overload a plug.
Never use something with a worn wire.
Never play with the wall socket.
Never let the wire go across a sink.

### Page 20

iron: screw, ship; plastic: bottle, beaker bowl;
cotton: shirt, socks, thread;
wood: chair, newspaper, window frame;
copper: pipe, pan; wool: hat, socks;
glass: window, beaker, bottle
Hard: iron, wood, copper, glass
Not rust: plastic, cotton, wood, wool, glass
Warm: cotton, wool.

### Page 21

**1** acorn; **2** conkers; **3** apples; **4** blown; **5** spins; **6** fur; **7** river; **8** mangoes; **9** small; **10** peaches.

### Page 22

Transparent: glass, water, cooking oil, coloured plastic, tissue paper.
Opaque: milk, china cup, coin, wood, leather glove, woollen rug, cotton tea towel.

### Page 23

**1** knitted clothes;
**2** flour; **3** clay; **4** table, chair or other wooden object; **5** milk.

### Page 24

The further the marble falls the deeper the dent it makes.
If the object is hard it makes a deeper dent than a soft one.
They should both land at the same time.
**1** large **2** large **3** large **4** small.

### Page 25

**1** yes; **2** yes; **3** yes; **4** no; **5** yes; **6** yes; **7** yes.

### Page 26

**1** easy; **2** hard; **3** hard; **4** easy; **5** hard; **6** easy; **7** hard.
Rubbing soap on the slope should reduce friction so objects will slip down the slope more easily.

### Page 27

**1** yes; **2** no; **3** no; **4** no; **5** no; **6** no; **7** yes.